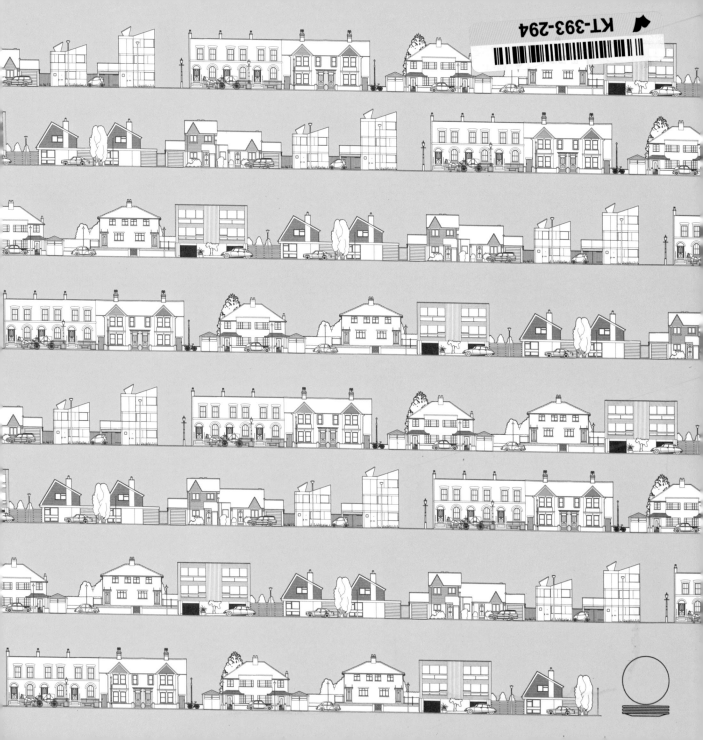

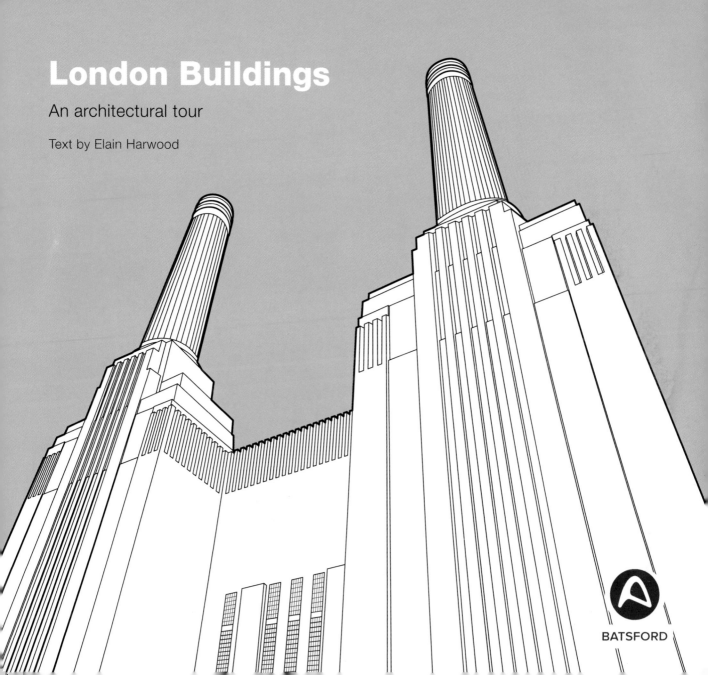

London Buildings

An architectural tour

Text by Elain Harwood

BATSFORD

for Ernö, Denys and their contemporaries,
whose work continues to challenge our
perceptions of beauty.

First published in the United Kingdom in 2011 by
Batsford, 10 Southcombe Street, London W14 0RA
An imprint of Anova Books Company Ltd

ISBN 9781849940238

A CIP catalogue record for this book is available from the British Library.

18 17 16 15 14 13 12 11
10 9 8 7 6 5 4 3 2 1

Text by Elain Harwood
Book Design by Lee-May Lim
Reproduction by Rival Colour Ltd, UK
Printed and bound by Toppan Leefung Printers Ltd, China

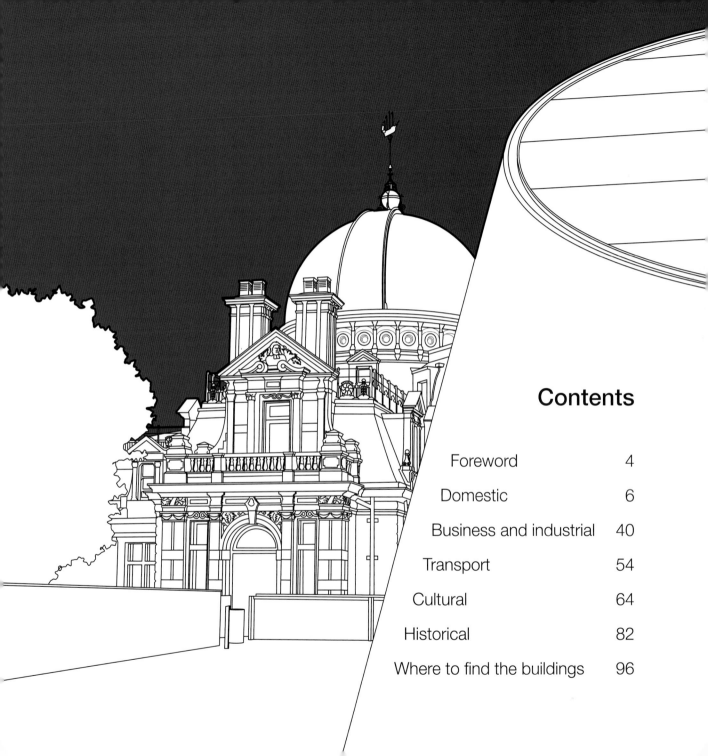

Contents

Foreword by Max Fraser

Like most cities, London holds up a plethora of architectural landmarks as cultural collateral. Tower Bridge, the Houses of Parliament, Westminster Abbey and the London Eye are just a handful of destination buildings that attract swarms of visitors. However, beyond the tourist hyperbole, this vast city has more unsung architectural heroes than are commonly known. There is a vast and diverse community of people which shares an appreciation for a great number of such buildings that don't conform to the common benchmarks of 'old, historic, or monumental'. In fact, somewhat unconsciously, lots of us grow quite attached to certain buildings that make up part of our everyday routine. Indeed, for many, architectural familiarity becomes a practical aid as one of the best navigation tools around London's complicated maze of streets.

Spread across the city are thousands of buildings that are symbolic of the era in which they were built. Not just bricks and mortar, each one tells a story of that particular moment in history before the speed of change or social, economic or political pressure pushed their significance into the background. Of course, architectural styles go in and out of vogue and many buildings have been demolished as a result.

More often than not, we do not mourn the many monstrosities that are eventually torn down. For example, the rash of sub-standard tower blocks that popped up across London in the 60s and 70s were not only eyesores on the skyline but also the subjects of an optimistic social experiment which broke down with time and caused decay to the very fabric of many areas.

That said, there are some valiant exceptions that have endured years of hatred but have ultimately tipped in people's favour, going on to become protected or even listed by local authorities. The 31-storey Trellick Tower (1972) is probably one of the more controversial examples of the Brutalist architectural movement, which has benefited from a wave of popularity over the past decade. The monolithic concrete structure looms high on west London's horizon and what was once home to the city's low-income families is now sought-after real estate, not least for its breathtaking views and proximity to gentrified Notting Hill.

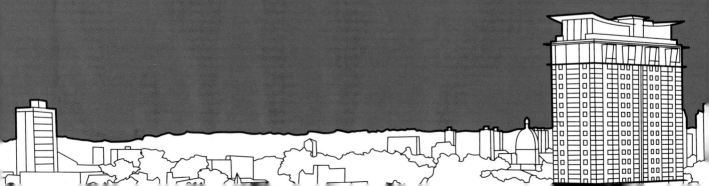

The various architectural examples that People Will Always Need Plates have highlighted in this book are representative of moments in time amid the ever-morphing neighbourhoods of the capital, be they on a domestic scale, such as the Isokon Building (1934), institutional, such as Royal Festival Hall (1951), public, such as Park Royal Underground station (1936) or monumental, such as Battersea Power Station (1935). People Will Always Need Plates has attracted a loyal following from people who have grown fond of their clean and confident illustrative reportage of such structures.

The duo behind the drawings – Hannah Dipper and Robin Farquhar – initially began their business in 2003 with a focus on the buildings that they love, namely Modernist examples from the 1930s as well as more monumental concrete structures of the 50s, 60s and 70s. Boasting clean rendered surfaces and large expanses of cast concrete as well as repeat patterns and simple logic, these buildings were graphic in form and devoid of much surface detailing or decoration, lending themselves perfectly to the rather purist illustrative style that has become signature for Dipper and Farquhar. While the buildings themselves may have deteriorated with years of London pollution and rain, People Will Always Need Plates view all their subjects through rose-tinted spectacles and aim to celebrate the core architectural elements in their colourful artworks.

Reproducing their fine-lined illustrations onto the medium of plates is a nod to the commemorative wares that have prevailed in the UK for several centuries. People Will Always Need Plates has revived this long tradition of illustrative plates and opened up their appeal to a new demographic – the aforementioned enthusiasts of our built environment. Crucially, however, the emphasis of their collections (be it plates, mugs, tea towels, placemats, bags etc) is on quality and usability, stemming from the duo's previous experiences in pragmatic design-consultancy jobs.

The illustrations featured in this book represent the architectural magnitude of certain key buildings that have been selected from across an urban area covering nearly 700 square miles. While London's better-known destinations of cultural significance are included, it is also refreshing to ponder the buildings that may have passed us by.

Not influenced by superfluous criteria, Dipper and Farquhar are simply editors of great architecture. As one turns the pages of this book, it is inevitable that your appreciation of the built environment, wherever you live, will be brought into sharper focus.

Max Fraser is a design commentator who works across the media of books, magazines, exhibitions, video, and events to broaden the conversation around contemporary design. He delivers content, commentary, and strategy for a variety of public and private bodies in the UK and abroad. He is the author of several design books including DESIGN UK and DESIGNERS ON DESIGN, which he co-wrote with Sir Terence Conran. More recently, he edited and published LONDON DESIGN GUIDE (www.londondesignguide.com)

www.peoplewillalwaysneedplates.co.uk

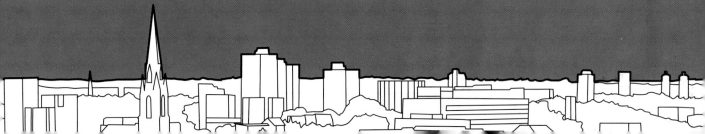

Trellick Tower

Architect: Ernő Goldfinger

1972

Goldfinger designed two towers for the London County Council that bookend the old county of London. To the east is Balfron Tower, smaller and squatter; to the west, in North Kensington, Trellick marked the end of public housing in towers. Inspired by Le Corbusier's unbuilt scheme for Algiers (1938–42), noisy lifts and rubbish chutes occupy the semi-detached tower, topped by the boiler house.

Wakeman Road, Kensal Green

Architect: Commissioned by freeholder,
All Souls College, Oxford

1880s–1900

The archetypal London terrace. There are miles
upon miles of these in a ring around the city,
including the large estates at Kensal Green
developed by All Souls College after 1880.
This one just happens to be a former People
Will Always Need Plates residence.

Great Arthur House

Architects: Chamberlin, Powell & Bon

1957

Great Arthur House is part of the Golden Lane
Estate, built for key workers in the City, hence its
buttercup-yellow curtain walling. At sixteen stories,
it was briefly London's tallest building. The distinctive
concrete roof conceals the lift mechanism and a
water tank, and there is a roof garden and pond,
designed for the tenants but closed in 1981.

Alton Estate (West)

Architects: London County Council
Architect's Department

1958

Alton West in Roehampton is a mixed development of old people's bungalows, houses, point blocks and slabs – housing for all ages – carefully planned to preserve a landscape by Capability Brown. Most famous are the slabs, inspired by Le Corbusier's Unité d'Habitation in Marseilles, but a similarly hard concrete aesthetic was adopted for the point blocks for single people and couples without children.

Highpoint I

Architects: Berthold Lubetkin and Tecton

1935

Lubetkin dreamed of building social housing, but
in the 1930s realised only middle-class flats in
extensive grounds on top of Highgate Hill. Two
cruciform blocks linked by a kidney-shaped foyer,
their clever massing of 2- and 3-bedroom units, with
separate maids' flats, and clean modern lines were
admired by Le Corbusier as a 'vertical garden city'.

Montevetro

Architects: Richard Rogers Partnership

2000

Built on the site of a former Hovis flour mill, right next to the Grade I-listed 18th-century church of St Mary at Battersea Reach, Montevetro is perhaps Rogers's strongest contribution to London's riverscape after his proposals for Coin Street were rejected. With its bathroom pods, manufactured in Denmark and craned into place, this building made prefabrication fashionable for luxury housing.

66 Frognal

Architects: Connell, Ward and Lucas

1937

Arguably the most sophisticated house by the leading modernist house designers of the 1930s, 66 Frognal, situated in Hampstead, is austere to the front, with balconies and a sun terrace to the rear, the latter later partly infilled with bedrooms. The masterpiece of Colin Lucas, it was restored in 2004 by Avanti Architects, who reintroduced the original colour scheme to the walls, which had long been painted white.

Kensal House

Architect: Maxwell Fry with Elizabeth Denby

1937

Kensal House in Ladbroke Grove was built by the Gas, Light and Coke Company as model low-cost housing, and made the reputations of Max Fry and housing expert Elizabeth Denby. The curved profiles, particularly of the related nursery, reflect the gasholders that were previously on the site. Each flat has two balconies, one in-set for drying clothes, the other for relaxing in the sun.

Keeling House

Architect: Denys Lasdun

1959

This Bethnal Green building was the original cluster block, narrow units set around a central service core, planned not to disturb the surrounding street pattern so you could chat across the balconies to your neighbours. It was one of Lasdun's first independent works, and the elevations are reminiscent of his master Berthold Lubetkin. It was restored in 2001 by Munkenbeck and Marshall.

Sun House

Architect: Maxwell Fry

1935

Just down the road from 66 Frognal in Hampstead, and less sophisticated but more curvaceous, is this evocatively named house, a projecting roof canopy providing a vertical contrast to the long, horizontal lines. The covered terrace at the end was perhaps a sleeping porch, an extreme example of the cult of outdoor living in the 1930s.

Isokon Building

Architect: Wells Coates
1934

Isokon, on Lawn Road, Hampstead, was developed by Coates and furniture manufacturer Jack Pritchard as minimum flats for young professionals – a trendy alternative to 'digs', with larger units for Pritchard and his children on the top. Residents included Walter Gropius and Agatha Christie. Henry Moore, Barbara Hepworth and Ben Nicholson were regulars at the Isobar restaurant added later. Renovated in 2003 by Avanti Architects.

Grand Union Walk

Architects: Nicholas Grimshaw & Partners

1988

These ten houses form a terrace facing the Regent's Canal in Camden Town. Most striking are the aluminium space-capsule facades, though these house mainly bedrooms – the double-height kitchen-diner is set back behind recessed glazing – while most of the construction is actually of concrete to keep out noise from Grimshaw's adjoining Sainsbury's supermarket.

Brunswick Centre

Architect: Patrick Hodgkinson

1972

The Brunswick Centre in Bloomsbury was a medium-rise, high-density alternative to the tower block. Originally intended as private housing with luxury shops, it was leased to the London Borough of Camden as a condition of its planning permission. The shopping centre was remodelled by Levitt Bernstein in 2005 and is now buzzing, while the flats have been painted as Hodgkinson intended.

Barbican: Cromwell Tower

Architects: Chamberlin, Powell & Bon

1973

Cromwell Tower is one of three triangular towers of 43 and 44 storeys built as landmarks to the Barbican, designed from 1955 onwards to return a residential population to the City. Oliver Cromwell was married in nearby St Giles, Cripplegate. The boat-like balconies were designed for wind resistance and the pick-hammered concrete surfaces responded to the monumental external load-bearing structure.

Shepton Court

Architects: London County Council
Architect's Department

1964

The original home of People Will Always Need
Plates, this is part of Battersea's Somerset Estate,
designed by Colin Lucas (one of the architects of 66
Frognal) and Peter Bottomley in 1961–2. The
strongly modelled blocks with their bands of
concrete and brick are foils to two 21-storey towers,
in a design earlier developed by the architects for
Bermondsey's Canada Estate.

Shirland Mews

Architects: Conran & Partners
2002

Shirland Mews is a modern interpretation in Maida Vale of the traditional London mews for Q Developments, fourteen crisply rendered houses set over dark-stained garaging. Each house features a combined kitchen and dining area raised half a level above an open-plan living area, cleverly detailed down to the open-tread stairs to maximize light. Speculative developments are rarely this elegant.

Maggie's Cancer Caring Centre, London

Architects: Rogers Stirk Harbour & Partners
2008

Winner of the 2009 RIBA Stirling Prize and London home to one of our favourite charities, set within Charing Cross Hospital in Hammersmith. Maggie's Centres were developed by Maggie Keswick, wife of architecture critic Charles Jencks, who died of breast cancer. Lord Rogers gave his design without fee, a double-height social space revolving around the kitchen like in his own Chelsea house, with consultation rooms off it.

Battersea Power Station

Architect: Sir Giles Gilbert Scott

1935 (A) & 1955 (B)

Celebrated by Pink Floyd, it's hard to imagine that there was originally just a rectangular block with two towers. Battersea Power Station was the first large power station in Britain, precursor of the national grid, and Scott was brought in to provide a decorative panache. Although long derelict, the A station (nearest the railway) retains its Art Deco control room.

One Canada Square

Architect: Cesar Pelli
1991

At 800 feet, One Canada Square is the tallest tower in Britain, yet this is masked by its great width, until you spot it from miles outside London. Its 3,960 windows are triple-glazed to improve its efficiency. It is the centrepiece of Canary Wharf, developed as a financial fortress by the Canadian firm Olympia and York.

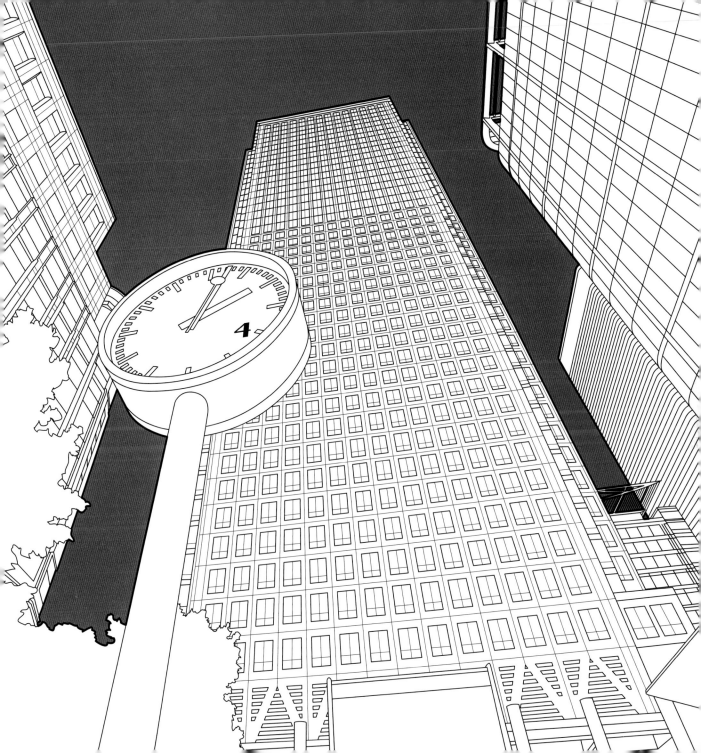

Butler's Wharf

Architects: James Tolley and Daniel Dale

1873

Butler's Wharf, near Tower Bridge, was once the largest warehouse complex on the Thames. When first built, it was the latest in industrial design, featuring fireproof floors, brick-vaulted basements and wrought iron roof trusses. After it closed in 1972 it was used as a video and performance art space, before it was redeveloped with flats and restaurants by Conran & Partners, 1992–2004.

Centre Point

Architect: Richard Seifert
1966

Centre Point, situated at the junction of Tottenham Court Road and New Oxford Street in the West End, has always been controversial. It was described by one architecture critic, Nikolaus Pevsner, as 'coarse' but was admired for its Op Art syncopation by another, Reyner Banham, as 'backing Britain'. It was novel for its prefabricated panels and construction from the inside out without cranes, and in 2009 the building won the Concrete Society's Mature Structures Award.

30 St Mary Axe

Architects: Foster & Partners

2004

Winner of the 2004 RIBA Stirling Prize and known as the Gherkin, this was built as the UK headquarters of re-insurers Swiss Re, who still lease space there. The shape was based on innovative computer modelling and features two layers of glazing to provide passive solar heating. All the glass panels are actually flat, save that at the very top.

Post Office Tower

Architects: Eric Bedford & G. R. Yeats for
the Ministry of Public Building and Works

1965

When more telephones were needed in the 1960s,
a tower with high frequency aerials resolved
problems of cabling in central London. Opened by
Tony Benn, then Postmaster General, the tower had
to be exceptionally stable to support the sensitive
equipment. This justified the addition of viewing
galleries and the Top of the Tower rotating
restaurant, originally run by Billy Butlin.

Gasholder No. 8

Built by the Imperial Gas Light
and Coke Company

1883

St Pancras had the most impressive array of
gasholder frames in Britain. No.8 and its neighbours,
called the 'Triplets' for their unique formation and in
storage since the building of the Channel Tunnel rail
link, have classical capitals in three tiers, and served
the deepest gas tanks ever constructed. Their
restoration will form part of the redevelopment of
King's Cross.

Rayners Lane Station

Architects: Reginald H. Uren under Adams,
Holden and Pearson

1938

Though built by New Zealander Reginald Uren,
Rayners Lane followed the generic modern brick
form established by Charles Holden for the 1930s
stations on the extended Piccadilly Line. It straddles
the pavement to make an unusually effective
landmark, with two shops tucked into the entrance.

By kind permission of Transport for London.

Vauxhall Bus Station

Architects: Kenneth Fraser, Robert Pugh, Daniel J Wong at Arup Associates
2004

A reorganization of this traffic gyratory enabled part of the road to be remodelled for buses. But an eye-catching design was needed, and a 200m long undulating stainless steel ribbon offers free and safe access while symbolizing movement and minimizing the need for foundations. 167 solar panels on the roof provide one-third of the bus station's electricity.

Park Royal Station

Architects: Herbert Welch & Felix Lander

1936

Welch and Lander were architects of the adjoining Haymills Estate of flats, houses, shops and a hotel, but Lander had previously worked for Charles Holden and the underground station clearly shows his influence. The massing of the tower, booking hall and stairs is particularly effective seen from the platforms.

By kind permission of Transport for London.

Waterloo Station

Architect: James Robb Scott for LSWR

1922

Waterloo Station was a mess, with some platforms sharing the same number, until in 1901 the London and South Western's Chief Engineer, J. W. Jacomb-Hood, studied station design in America. The result was Britain's first terminus in which the concourse was more important than the train shed, the latter a picturesque lattice of glazed roofs rather than a soaring arch.

Thames Barrier

Architects: Rendel, Palmer and Tritton for the GLC

1982

This is the world's second-largest movable flood barrier, raised when high tides threaten London. It spans the Thames between Silvertown on the north bank and Charlton to the south, and was made possible when London's docks moved downstream to Tilbury. There were four closures in the 1980s, 35 in the 1990s and 75 in the 2000s. Originally designed to protect London until 2030, revised estimates of sea-level rise have extended its lifespan to 2060–70.

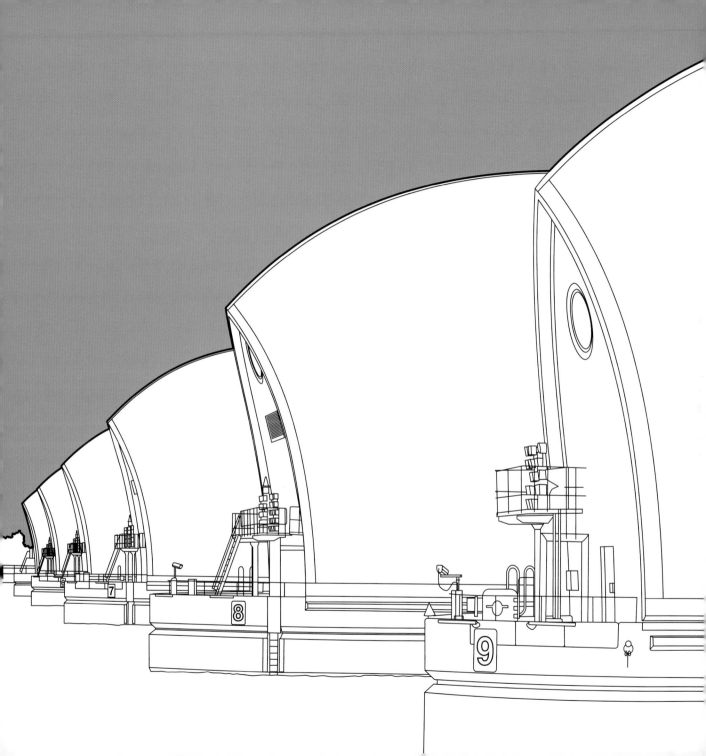

Dulwich Picture Gallery

Architect: Sir John Soane

1814

Soane's design of a series of interlinked rooms
naturally lit through skylights has influenced art
gallery design ever since. To the west were originally
almshouses, now adapted as additional galleries,
but the centrepiece remains an eerie mausoleum
housing the remains of Sir Francis Bourgeois and
Noel Desenfans, who amassed the original collection
for the King of Poland.

Hayward Gallery

Architects: Norman Engleback et al, London
County Council/Greater London Council
Architect's Department

1968

The low bunker was conceived in 1957–60 to
counter the bulk of the Royal Festival Hall, situated
next door on the South Bank, while the walkway
concealed car parking; Warren Chalk, Ron Herron
and Dennis Crompton, later members of Archigram,
worked on the details. The kinetic light sculpture by
Dante Leonelli on the roof responds to wind force
and was retained from the Continuum exhibition
of 1971.

Victoria and Albert Museum

Architect: Aston Webb
(final arrangement and façade)

1909 (to buildings of 1856–73)

The first Director, Sir Henry Cole, described
the Museum in 1857 as 'a refuge for destitute
collections'. More than a century later, Sir Roy
Strong called it 'an extremely capacious handbag'.
It grew out of the success of the Great Exhibition
of 1851. The courtyard, rear galleries and restaurant
were built by military engineers and decorated by
art students.

National Theatre

Architect: Sir Denys Lasdun
1976

Lasdun's design was first conceived to sit next to County Hall, with an opera house as well as a theatre. The Olivier Theatre remains London's finest open stage.

'...A clever way of building a nuclear power station in the middle of London without anyone objecting.' (The Prince of Wales).

'We love it!' (People Will Always Need Plates)

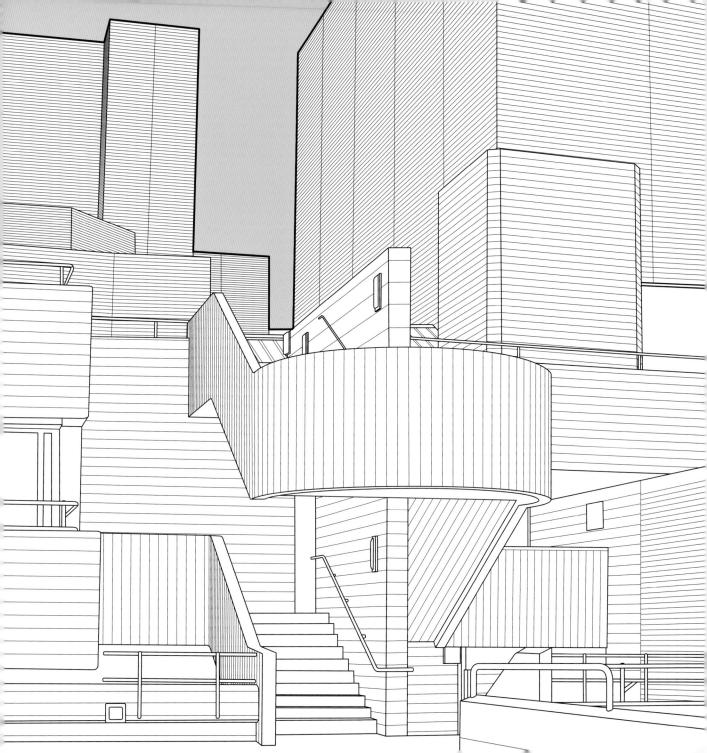

Commonwealth Institute

Architects Stirrat Johnson-Marshall, Peter
Newnham and Roger Cunliffe of RMJM

1962

A showcase for the emerging Commonwealth, this
building in Kensington was conceived as a 'tent in
the park' where every nation's stand could be seen
from the central entrance. In this it resembled the
plan of the Dome of Discovery at the Festival of
Britain in 1951. Its hyperbolic paraboloid roof was
engineered by James Sutherland and made using 25
tonnes of copper donated by what is now Zambia.

Saatchi Gallery:
Duke of York's HQ

Architect: John Sanders

1801

Originally built as the Royal Military Asylum, a school
for the children of soldiers' widows. It later became
the headquarters of the Duke of York's regiment.
Behind the striking frontage with its sturdy Roman
Doric portico, this Chelsea building was remodelled
and extended in 2008 by Paul Davis & Partners and
Allford Hall Monaghan Morris as the Saatchi Gallery.

Royal Ballet School: Bridge of Aspiration

Architects: Wilkinson Eyre
2003

The bridge links premises for the Upper School, in Floral Street, Covent Garden, to the Royal Ballet Company's own studios in the adjacent Royal Opera House – hence the name. 23 square portals rotate through 90° to form a concertina-like glazed structure. Designed by computer with engineers Flint and Neill, the prefabricated spine of aluminium, chosen for its lightness, was assembled in two hours.

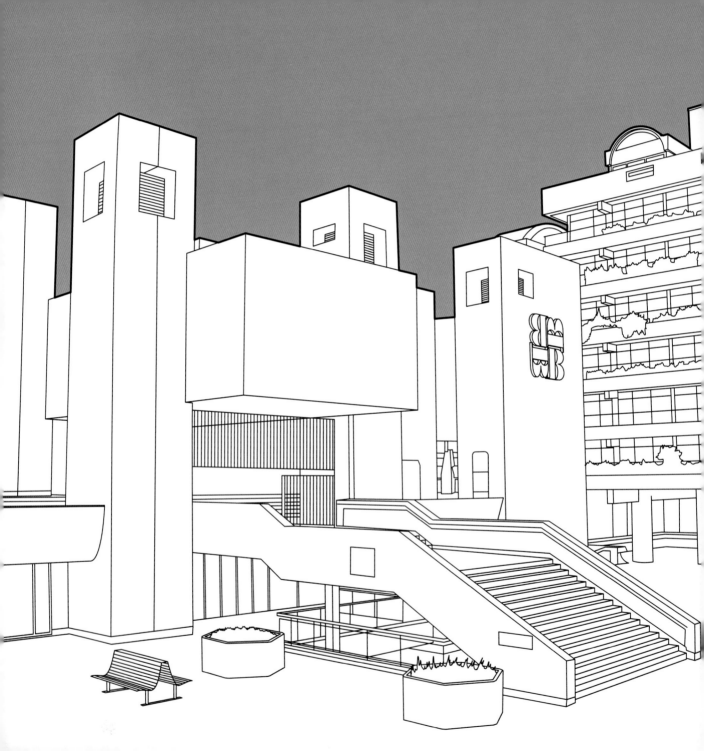

Barbican Centre

Architects: Chamberlin, Powell & Bon

1982

This is the largest arts centre in Europe, with a theatre, concert hall, art gallery, library and cinemas, but was planned in this form only after the adjoining tower blocks were under construction. Hence half of the building is sunk into the ground, the lowest floor 17 feet below sea level. The theatre is most dramatic, with no aisles inside the auditorium.

Royal Festival Hall

Architects: Robert Matthew, Leslie Martin, Peter Moro et al, London County Council Architect's Department

1951

How could the Festival of Britain celebrate our culture without a concert hall? One was built on the South Bank in just three years, a formidable achievement at a time when materials were still rationed. The exterior was remodelled in 1964 but the interior, by Moro and his ex-students, remains little altered, the auditorium an 'egg in a box' to shield it from surrounding traffic noise.

Royal Observatory, Greenwich & Peter Harrison Planetarium (foreground)

Architects: Sir Christopher Wren / Allies & Morrison

1675–6, 2007

At Wren's Royal Observatory, on the site of a little castle which may have inspired the romantic design, measurements were made that established accurate data for longitude in the eighteenth century and made Greenwich the Prime Meridian in 1884. The 45-ton, bronze-clad truncated cone, tilted at 51.5° to the horizontal, the latitude of Greenwich, houses a 120-seat planetarium.

Cumberland Place

Architect: John Nash
1830s

John Nash was architect to the Prince Regent, later George IV and Britain's greatest royal architectural patron. He laid out Regent's Park, Regent Street and Waterloo Place, as well as the garden front of Buckingham Palace. Cumberland Place forms part of the ring of grand houses and terraces that surround the park, more palatial than the work at the Palace.

St John's Gate

Architects: W. P. Griffiths, R. Norman Shaw & J. Oldrid Scott
1504

Built for Prior Thomas Docwra, this Clerkenwell building became a printing works and pub until it was acquired in 1874 by the revived Most Venerable Order of St John as its headquarters and museum, and of its offshoot, the St. John Ambulance. It was much restored, most thoroughly in 1885–6 by John Oldrid Scott, who added offices and a Chapter House (1901–4).

Sir John Soane's Museum

Architect: Sir John Soane

1794, 1812 & 1824

Soane's house in Lincoln's Inn Fields not only contained his home and office, but also increasingly eclectic collections of paintings, drawings and sculpture. The alabaster sarcophagus of Seti I lies in what Soane called the 'Sepulchral Chamber'. He held a three-day party on its arrival. Soane wanted the house to strike the visitor's soul with 'as vivid an emotion as a Beethoven quartet'.

The Queen's House

Architect: Inigo Jones
1617

Jones was the first British architect known to travel extensively in Italy, and introduced the classical style of Andrea Palladio, the model for major country houses here thereafter. The Queen's House is classically correct, and its main rooms are properly on the first floor, but curiously it was built over the road, a bridge between Greenwich Palace and the park.

The Pump House

Built by James and William Simpson
1861

Originally built by the Simpsons, father and son, as a pumping station to supply water to the lake and cascades in Battersea Park, first laid out in 1854, the little brick Pump House was transformed in 1988–92 by Rod McAllister into a gallery, revamped again in 1995 and was the venue for the authors' wedding in 2006.

Geffrye Museum

Built by the Ironmongers' Company

1714

One of London's finest almshouse complexes is that built by Sir Robert Geffrye for the Worshipful Company of Ironmongers in 1712–14 in Shoreditch, probably with Robert Burford as builder. It was converted to a furniture museum in 1912–13 by the LCC to inspire local craftsmen. A wing for twentieth-century displays and a restaurant was added, to designs by Branson Coates, in 1995–8.

Where to find the buildings